Gone Forever!
Sabretooth

Rupert Matthews

Heinemann Library
Chicago, Illinois

© 2003 Heinemann Library
a division of Reed Elsevier Inc.
Chicago, Illinois

Customer Service 888-454-2279
Visit our website at www.heinemannlibrary.com

Designed by Ron Kamen and Paul Davies & Associates
Illustrations by Maureen and Gordon Gray, James Field (SGA), and Darren Lingard
Originated by Ambassador Litho Ltd.
Printed and bound in China by South China Printing Company

07 06 05 04
10 9 8 7 6 5 4 3 2

Library of Congress Cataloging-in-Publication Data
Matthews, Rupert.
  Sabretooth / Rupert Matthews.
     p. cm. -- (Gone forever)
Summary: Describes what has been learned about the physical features, behavior, and surroundings of the long-extinct sabretooth.
Includes bibliographical references and index.
  ISBN 1-40340-791-6 (HC), 1-4034-3419-0 (Pbk.)
  1. Sabertooth--Juvenile literature. [1. Sabertooth tigers. 2. Prehistoric animals.] I. Title. II. Gone forever (Heinemann Library)
  QE882.C15 M37 2003
  569'.75--dc21
                    2002003752

Acknowledgments
The author and publishers are grateful to the following for permission to reproduce copyright material:
pp. 4, 12, 22 Natural History Museum, London; p. 6 Bettman/Corbis; p 8 Lester V. Bergman/Corbis; p. 10 Science VU/Visuals Unlimited; p. 14 Tom McHugh/Science Photo Library; p. 16 Nature Picture Library; p. 18 A. J. Copley/Visuals Unlimited; p, 20 Sinclair Stammers/Science Photo Library; p. 24 P. Morris/Ardea; p. 26 Charles H. Coles/American Museum of Natural History. Cover photograph reproduced with permission of Science Photo Library.

Every effort has been made to contact copyright holders of any material reproduced in this book. Any omissions will be rectified in subsequent printings if notice is given to the publisher.
Special thanks to Dr. Peter Mackovicky for his review of this book.

Some words are shown in bold, **like this.** You can find out what they mean by looking in the glossary.

Contents

Gone Forever!

About 25 thousand years ago, many kinds of giant animals lived around the world. Most of these animals are now **extinct.** This means they have all died. Scientists find out about them by studying their **fossils.**

One of these extinct animals was the sabretooth. The sabretooth was a large cat that hunted other animals. It was named sabretooth because of its long, sharp teeth. These were shaped like a **sabre,** a type of curved sword.

Sabretooth's Home

There is a place in California called La Brea. Here, there are **tar pits** where plants and animals were trapped many years ago. Scientists study the plants and animal bones they find there. These **fossils** tell scientists what the area was like when the sabretooth lived.

The **valley** where the tar pits were formed was dry and warm. Grass covered the ground and there were only a few trees. In summer the weather could get very hot. In winter it was not very cold.

7

The Tar Pits

Many bones of the sabretooth and other animals have been found in the **tar pits.** The **tar** was often covered with water. Animals that came to drink got caught in the tar and could not escape.

This is a model of a trapped mammoth in a tar pit.

Sabretooths sometimes tried to eat the animals
stuck in the tar. Often, they got stuck in the tar,
too. Their bones were added to all the others
already trapped there.

Plants

The seeds and leaves trapped in the **tar pits** tell scientists about the plants that grew when the sabretooth lived. Scientists also study how many seeds there are of each kind. This tells them which plants were the most common.

fossil of a seed

10

Grasses were the most common type of plant at the time of the sabretooth. There were also some trees. Animals that ate grasses and animals that ate trees have been found in the tar pits.

11

Living with the Sabretooth

The **fossil** bones of other animals have been found in the **tar pits.** Some of these bones belonged to an animal called the **ground sloth.** They tell us what the ground sloth was like when it was alive.

The ground sloth was a big, powerful animal. It weighed about as much as two cars. It was so long it could have touched a basketball rim when it stood up. The ground sloth had huge claws on its front feet and it ate grass and other plants.

What Was the Sabretooth?

Many bones of the sabretooth have been found in the **tar pits** and in other places. The bones show what the sabretooth looked like. They show that the sabretooth was a large type of cat.

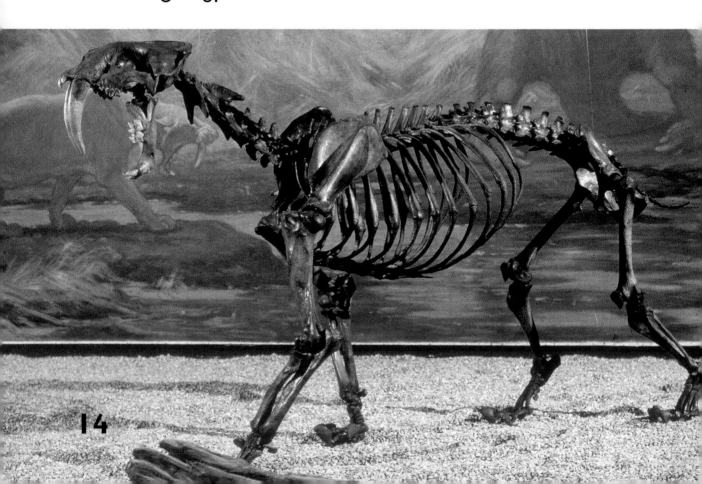

The sabretooth was a very strong animal. It had powerful front legs and paws with sharp claws. It was probably not a very fast runner. The sabretooth would creep up on its **prey** and kill it with its teeth and claws.

Growing Up

Scientists think that baby sabretooths were like lion and tiger cubs today. They did not have the same long teeth as the adults. They could not win a fight with other hunting animals. They may have hidden in long grass.

This is a modern lion cub.

Baby sabretooths were probably guarded by the adults. Several females may have lived together. One would look after the young while the others hunted. The young would have spent lots of time playing with each other.

Learning to Hunt

As a young sabretooth got bigger, it grew long teeth and strong muscles. By the age of six months, a young sabretooth was almost an adult. It began to hunt its own food.

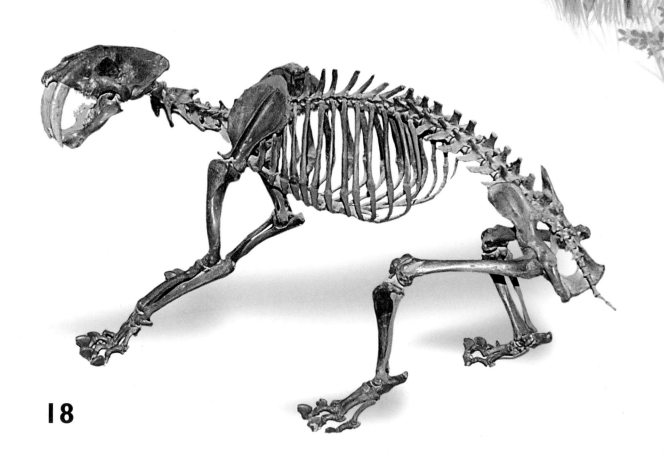

At first, young sabretooths would hunt with their mothers. The adults taught the young how to move and hide in tall grass. This is how sabertooths would creep up on their **prey.**

Sabre Teeth

The sabretooth was given its name because of the two long teeth in its upper jaw. These teeth had sharp points. The sabretooth's teeth were **jagged,** like a knife.

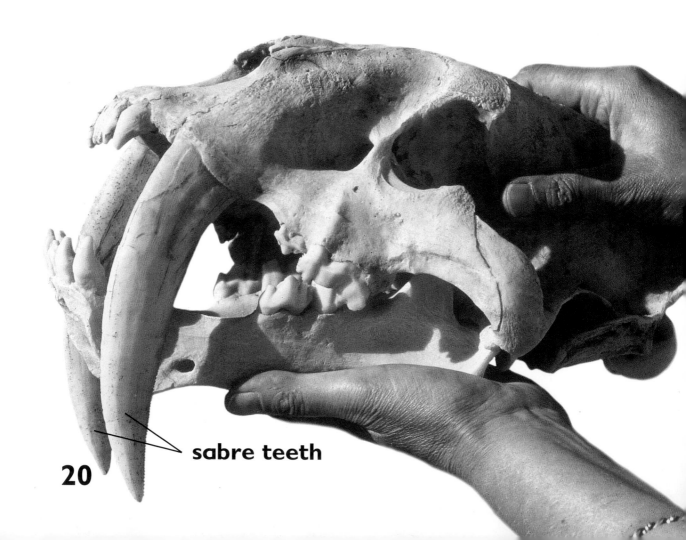

sabre teeth

20

The sabretooth used its long teeth to kill its **prey.**
The cat would knock its prey to the ground and
hold it down with its front legs. Then it would bite
the prey with its long teeth and kill it.

Sabre Attack!

The back legs of the sabretooth were short and strong. **Fossil** bones show that these legs had very powerful muscles. The sabretooth used its back legs to leap forward quickly.

When hunting, the sabretooth would creep as close as it could to its **prey.** Then it would dart forward to catch its prey before it could run away.

Sabretooth's Prey

The bones of the **prey** eaten by the sabretooth have been found in the **tar pits.** These show that the sabretooth hunted large, plant-eating animals. They ate animals such as the imperial **mammoth,** horses, and **bison.**

imperial
mammoth
skeleton

mammoth

horses

bison

The sabretooth liked to hunt large animals. One large animal would give it plenty of meat to eat. But mammoths were very big and strong. The sabretooth probably only ate mammoths that were stuck in the **tar.**

Dire Wolves

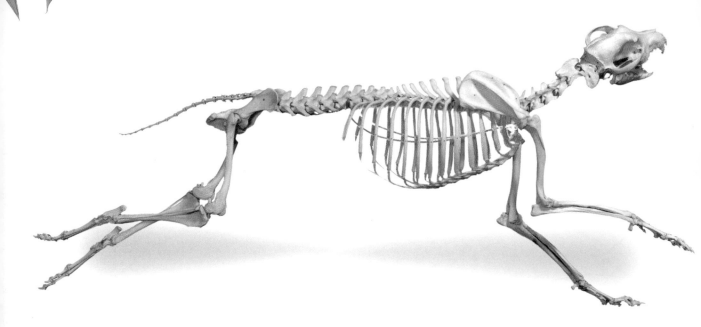

Other hunting animals lived at the same time as the sabretooth. One of these was the **dire wolf.** The dire wolf was about as big as a wolf of today. It may have hunted its **prey** by chasing it for long distances.

Sometimes, dire wolves would steal a meal from the sabretooths. Dire wolves were smaller than sabretooths. But if there were enough of them, they could join together to drive sabretooths away from their food.

Where Did the Sabertooth Live?

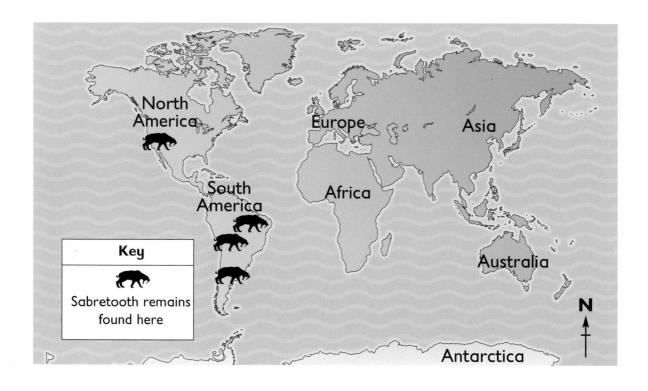

The sabretooth lived in North and South America. It roamed across open grasslands. Different kinds of cats with sabre teeth lived in other parts of the world, too.

When Did the Sabretooth Live?

The sabretooth lived between about one million and 15,000 years ago. This means it lived in what scientists call the Ice Age.

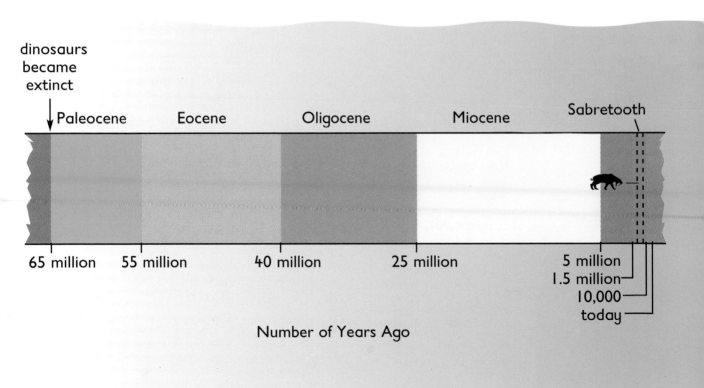

dinosaurs became extinct

Paleocene   Eocene   Oligocene   Miocene   Sabretooth

65 million   55 million   40 million   25 million   5 million
1.5 million
10,000
today

Number of Years Ago

Fact File

Sabretooth	
Length:	7 feet (2.2 meters)
Weight:	880 pounds (400 kilograms)
Time:	Pleistocene, about one million to 15,000 years ago
Place:	North and South America

How to Say It

mammoth—maam-uth
sabre—say-ber

Glossary

bison plant-eating mammal, like a large hairy cow

dire wolf type of wolf that was larger and stronger than modern wolves

extinct no longer living on Earth

fossil remains of a plant or animal, usually found in rocks. Most fossils are hard parts like bones, teeth, and seeds. Some fossils are traces of animals, such as their footprints.

ground sloth plant-eating animal. It lived in North and South America at the same time as the sabretooth.

jagged sharp edge with with many tiny zigzags along its length. The cutting edge of a steak knife is jagged.

mammoth type of elephant that lived at the same time as the sabretooth.

prey animal that is hunted and eaten by other animals

sabre type of long, curved sword once used by soldiers

tar black, sticky liquid. Tar bubbles up from the ground in some places.

tar pit place where tar comes to the surface from deep underground

valley low area of land found between hills and mountains

31

More Books to Read

Goecke, Michael P. *Saber-Toothed Cat.* Edina, Minn.: Abdo & Daughters, 2003.

Goecke, Michael P. *Dire Wolf.* Edina, Minn.: Abdo & Daughters, 2003.

An older person can help you read this book.

Hehner, Barbara. *Ice Age Sabretooth: All About the Most Ferocious Cat That Ever Lived.* New York: Crown Publishers, 2002.

Index